SUCKED IN!

EXPERIENCING HEAVENLY HELP AT THE DEVIL'S HOLE

LINDSEY (BURGESS) WAGGONER

WESTBOW
PRESS®
A DIVISION OF THOMAS NELSON
& ZONDERVAN

Copyright © 2020 Lindsey (Burgess) Waggoner.

All rights reserved. No part of this book may be used or reproduced by any means, graphic, electronic, or mechanical, including photocopying, recording, taping or by any information storage retrieval system without the written permission of the author except in the case of brief quotations embodied in critical articles and reviews.

This book is a work of non-fiction. Unless otherwise noted, the author and the publisher make no explicit guarantees as to the accuracy of the information contained in this book and in some cases, names of people and places have been altered to protect their privacy.

WestBow Press books may be ordered through booksellers or by contacting:

WestBow Press
A Division of Thomas Nelson & Zondervan
1663 Liberty Drive
Bloomington, IN 47403
www.westbowpress.com
844-714-3454

Because of the dynamic nature of the Internet, any web addresses or links contained in this book may have changed since publication and may no longer be valid. The views expressed in this work are solely those of the author and do not necessarily reflect the views of the publisher, and the publisher hereby disclaims any responsibility for them.

Any people depicted in stock imagery provided by Getty Images are models, and such images are being used for illustrative purposes only. Certain stock imagery © Getty Images.

ISBN: 978-1-6642-1388-3 (sc)
ISBN: 978-1-6642-1389-0 (e)

Library of Congress Control Number: 2020923353

Print information available on the last page.

WestBow Press rev. date: 11/30/2020

To all who may read my story of fear, conviction, and salvation through a harrowing trial in life, the words I leave you:

> Never ever let your hope and faith in God die. Keep hoping until hope dies; remember, however, that hope never dies. God is never an uncaring Father. The most important thing we can ever have from Him whilst we live is the gift of life we have. We must never ever trade it for anything else!
>
> —Ernest Agyemang Yeboah

CONTENTS

Introduction ix

Before the Fall. 1
Two Steps Forward, One Step Back. 5
Until Death Do Us Part 9
The New Normal 13
Changes 16
A Newfound Love. 20
New York, New York. 23
The Day 26
Leaving on a Jet Boat 30
All the Right Calls 34
Back to St. Louie. 40

INTRODUCTION

July 18, 2011, was a day that forever changed my life. I experienced excitement, peril, hopelessness, fear, peace, death, and life all in a matter of hours. This book tells my true life experience that rattled my security in God, in myself, and in my future—and placed it securely under my feet as my foundation for holding onto the only faith I will ever need. Niagara Falls in New York may be one of the most beautiful wonders of the planet, but it is also one of the most deadly. For this day in 2011, it proved to be just that for me. However, unlike any other person who has fallen into the Niagara River without a life jacket or safety harness, without knowledge of the ugly turmoil underneath the gorgeous waves of beauty that flow so vigorously down the channel of the river, I was able to come out alive. I survived and was eternally changed in my perspective of our human existence. We all have a purpose.

BEFORE THE FALL

It's funny how when we are young, we don't really see the entire parade of life. We don't recognize the importance of those small moments that make up the bigger moments in our lives. We don't appreciate people who come and go during our journey or know why they were ever playing a part in it.

That was me before July 18, 2011. My life had taken so many different twists and turns already, and I just kept swirling around in my issues. People want to throw around karma as an excuse for why their lives seem so miserable, but it is truly a result of our own decisions. What many people don't know about my story is that I've had more than one flirtation with death. In fact, I have been flirting with death for years and haven't wanted to acknowledge that truth about myself.

As a child, I was always a pleaser. I wanted to impress people, and I wanted to satisfy my parents. If I was told to jump, I replied, "How high?" I was a perfectionist, and I began obsessing over situations out of my control. I would have anxiety about being accepted and liked. I began a ritualistic lifestyle of obsessively cleaning and making things "perfect." But my life was not perfect;

I was not perfect. I had physical traits and deformities that I did not like. I hated them. I would pray at night to have those things removed from myself. I was teased throughout my intermediate years in school and would get physically ill just thinking about going to school. Why were people so cruel?

I was a tomboy. I liked sports, and I found that I had some sort of identity in sports. My dad was my best friend, and he gave me a sense of security with his role in my life. I knew he loved me and wanted the best for me. So I adopted a sportsman's mentality and gained some confidence; however, things were still not perfect. I was still not good enough. I was a bit on the heavy side, and comments would come and go, but it was something that always danced around in the back of my mind. *Why can't I be slim and cute like the other girls in high school? If I were thin, I would be happier.*

One day, that thought grew into a cancerous tumor called an eating disorder. After a volleyball teammate made a rude comment about my "fat behind," I realized I must lose weight no matter what the cost. I would do whatever it took to slim down. With my already perfectionistic mindset, it was going to happen. What started out as an innocent diet developed into a life-destroying monster. Praise and compliments, unbeknownst to me or anyone else, invited a greedy mindset in which a limit was never enough. Less was always more with weight.

Fast-forward a few years. I met a man—I will call him Ben—who would become my first husband. I did not know how to love myself, and I was hiding my monster in my closet of secrets about my true self. How could I ever truly love him? I couldn't, and I didn't. I loved the fact that he was an escape from my parents' honesty and the harsh truth they dished out about my disordered lifestyle with food. I knew with him I could relish my disordered eating and maintain that lifestyle, and he would never know the truth. The truth always comes out, though.

He discovered the ugly demon I was protecting so carefully, and he began to peel back the onion. I was losing more and more weight and reached a devastatingly low point when I decided to go to a modeling scouting call that I had heard about on the radio. As I waltzed up to the agents, they looked at my five-foot-ten frame and all 105 pounds of me. They smiled and seemed pleased. I was not sure about how much they valued my attempts at being model-thin until the next morning, when I got a phone call that I had been accepted. Thrilled, I jetted to the golf course to find my husband and tell him. He was not as happy as I was. He knew the dangerous path I was already treading and could see it getting even worse. I was very sick.

I was working at a local doctor's office. As I announced my big news and dreams of being an aspiring model, I knew something was about to change. An intervention was about to happen. I was given ultimatums to save my life. They would not participate in allowing me to slowly kill myself—to slowly starve my body to death. I was forced into treatment. I was more concerned with finishing my photo shoot with the agency than I was with living to see another month.

I spent two months in an inpatient facility in Arizona. It was traumatic, to say the least. I walked in and saw tubes out of noses and veins bursting out of girls' bodies, with bulging rib cages and joints. I did not need to be there. In my mind, I was in control of who I was and in control of my weight, and I could stop at any point. But I didn't want to stop. I had so much time in my life to "get back to normal." So I thought.

I tried to sign myself out and fly home. The doctors said they doubted I would make it home alive in my current condition. They said I was the most stubborn patient there. Although I still question the legitimacy of that, I do know I was extremely honest about my manipulative disorder. I cared so little about being able to spend time off the facility grounds with my husband by eating all my food and fulfilling all requirements toward the commitment to get healthier. I chose the disorder over him, over myself, over everything, and over everyone. I would rather be in control of everything. But at twenty-one, I didn't realize I was in control of nothing. I would learn this lesson hardcore at age thirty.

TWO STEPS FORWARD, ONE STEP BACK

The treatment facility offered a Christian-based program, and I was immersed in church and praise services, prayer, and counseling groups with a God-centered mindset. Being raised in church and professing my faith at age eight, being baptized, and attending church every Sunday morning and night until I was able to drive did not affect me at the treatment center. I was literally numb to it all. I enjoyed the atmosphere, and I did love the music, but I was disconnected. I was so focused on trying to block people from trying to control me. All my life, I had felt that other people were trying to tamper with my success and manipulate me. Although I was wrong in my assumptions, I still carried that attitude.

Finally, the day came after two months of being separated from the world as I knew it. I was able to go home. I was so relieved and could not wait to have a fresh start. While I was in treatment, my husband at the time had moved us to a brand-new apartment. I feared the former apartment was toxic and would only refresh bad memories of indulging in my behaviors. A new place would be perfect for engaging in a healthier lifestyle. I found out that a new place, a new location, and a new set of walls was not the cure. It didn't make the problem magically disappear.

I was participating in food binges and taking shopping trips to Walmart at three in the morning. On and on the manic behaviors and lack of control went. When I came home in September 2002, I was around 110 pounds. By November of that year, I was 165 pounds. Sounds great on my five-foot-ten frame, but I was a chaotic mess of depression, envy, and fear. I panicked and knew I had a lot of weight I had to lose as soon as possible. So I reached back into my trusty toolbox of disorderly conduct with food, and I decided this time I would try living on orange juice for as long as possible. I managed to get back down to 115 pounds. Such a relief to be in control again! One morning, I went to use the restroom. I sat down and realized I was unable to go. Why couldn't I go when I could feel my bladder's urgent need for relief? When I tried to stand up, I felt a massive pinch in my lower back, and I was stuck in a contorted position crying out for help. "Ben! Help me! I cannot move, and I cannot use the bathroom!" He rushed me to the emergency room. Upon seeing the doctor, I was told it was a miracle I was not already dead. My potassium levels were so incredibly low that most people were already having heart attacks at that point. Normal potassium levels are typically around 3.5 millimoles per liter. Mine were lower than 2.5 millimoles per liter.

I was treated at the hospital for three days and found out I needed surgery to remove the massive kidney stones I had developed. My hands were stuck in a contorted state of muscle cramps, and I was physically exhausted. My parents were in a state of hopelessness as to my disordered mind and were habitually praying to God for an intervention. My psychiatrist wanted to send me to a city hospital for further treatment. I agreed, and when it came time to sign on the dotted line, Ben questioned everything. Thankfully, because of his intuition, I did not sign my life away to them. If I had signed, I would have spent several years there before being released back into society. It was basically a mental institution. I still feel such gratitude to him for what he did for me that day.

Upon my return home, I was released from my place of work, and that was definitely a blessing in disguise. I needed to go back and finish my college degree pursuits. I dabbled in the medical environment, sales, and working at local stores; nothing seemed to fulfill my potential and use what I feel are my strengths. I fought with myself for a while, and finally I gave in and decided to move onward with my aspirations to become a teacher. I realized, as I moved along through the coursework, that school was something that I always felt "good" at doing. I felt committed to my schooling and felt at home with my community of school personnel and classmates. I assumed only would I feel that way more strongly as a part of the faculty of a school in which I belonged.

I graduated in 2006 with a degree in early childhood education and quickly gained my first teaching job. I was so invested in being a good teacher and so excited to have a role in children's lives. My disordered thoughts were still in my mind, just placed back into a closet and tucked away because I finally felt I had something to live for and goals to meet. I was motivated to be successful at something other than being in control of my physiology. I truly realized how much I love school and kids. I wanted to help those kids that felt like I did when I was their age.

I wanted to give so much love to those that didn't feel loved. I wanted to change their perspective on life and school. I still want those same things as a teacher. I don't think those aspirations ever leave you as an educator.

After three years of loving teaching and the community of colleagues around me, I was smacked with a devastating blow on May 23, 2009.

UNTIL DEATH DO US PART

There is something eerie about the memories that stick with us for a lifetime all because of one tragic moment in life. The day I first encountered death addressing my immediate family, attacking my home and knocking down the stable walls that surrounded me, was a day I will never forget, from the time I awoke until the time I lay down, attempting to rest.

It was the first day of my summer vacation as a teacher. The school year had ended the day prior, and I was waking up to a beautiful, sunny Saturday morning. I heard the birds chirping and the lawn mower outside my window. That school year had been devastatingly tough, as I had gone through a divorce from my husband of seven years. My parents had been my stability throughout the whole process, and walking away from a new home, only taking my personal things and a lot of accrued debt, was not satisfying. However, my parents opened their arms, and my childhood home was now my adult home, too. It was a humbling experience for me, but as the months carried on, I began to realize it was not so bad living there with them again. I realized how much I was loved and how much I had missed the relationship I had with my parents. Throughout the marriage, my disorder and my true feelings about the reason I was married to him became a festering sore. I was not happy for a long time, and neither was Ben. So we agreed to part ways, and I wanted to try to have a new start on living life.

My dad was always such a comfort and hero in my life. I know many people feel that way about their fathers, and I was not any different. I will never forget the time I was selling my jewelry after my divorce to use the money to pay off debt. I went from one pawn shop to another, trying to get the best value for my possessions. Finally, I realized I was only going to get a couple hundred dollars. I asked my dad if he could take it for me, as I had to work the next day and I honestly just felt too humiliated to do it. I thought he would be able to squeeze out more cash for me as well. I came home the following day, and there on my bed was a bag of money from the jewelry. That was my dad every day for me. Doing all those little things, and sometimes big things, just to make my life easier.

I began to notice he was not looking so well the last couple of months before he left us. I would be talking as I sat and graded papers and peer over at him, and he would be sleeping so deeply. I would think to myself, *He was just awake a second ago?* I noticed that he was not eating as much when Mom brought his meals to him. He was working every day, sweating a lot when he worked, and typically he would eat a big portion of whatever she made. He was eating only a fraction. Yet, what became more alarming was his weight. He was getting heavier and more bloated. He was zoning out a lot. But I chalked it up to the fact that he was fifty years old, thinking that is just what getting older is about. I remember shortly before school ended that year, I came home from school, put my purse and bags down in my old childhood room, and thought to myself, *I am actually feeling happy. I don't have a lot of things to try to make me happy, but I am happy.* That was a pinnacle moment for me. In my marriage, I had bought a lot of things to support an artificial happiness. It didn't work. After the divorce, I began to see how much I had shut out relationships and people who actually created a genuine happiness. I feel God created us that way. That is why people always say that things cannot buy you happiness.

Everything was normal for the most part on that day, and Mom and Dad had been taking care of errands and cutting grass all morning. Somehow, they got into an argument that persisted throughout the afternoon. So my mom got on the phone, and my dad went to the treadmill in the other room, I assume to let off steam. I heard the treadmill running in the other room, and it would sound as if my dad was stopping intermittently during his running session. Then I heard it stop. The next noise I heard was the crashing sound in the kitchen and my mother yelling for me. My immediate assumption was that I had done something wrong and was "in trouble" for it. But what was that sound? The refrigerator falling over was my guess. I walked into the kitchen and saw my father lying face-down on the floor. The back of his shorts was wet, and obviously he had hit the floor hard. My mom told me anxiously that he had passed out, which was an occurrence for many years because of his blood sugar. He was not eating right, and I remember several occasions of his dieting fiascos when he passed out in place, but he would regain consciousness and eat, and life would go back to normal for him. He was having a seizure, so we thought, and knowing that moving him over was not a safe thing to do, we tried to let his seizure pass. He had struck his face on the counter pretty hard and was bleeding. We needed to turn him but were not comfortable doing so until the seizure succumbed. I started to notice his neck was turning blue. At that point, we then forced ourselves to turn him over, and the glassy look of his eyes seared me. He was not just having a seizure. He had had a massive heart attack. Not knowing CPR, my mom began yelling outside to our neighbors, who came darting over to help. They were familiar with CPR and began the process. I called 911, and we waited. My aunts, who are registered nurses, came rushing over as well. They were not hopeful. The ambulance was at the house for what seemed like forever. Finally, they got Dad inside and basically cruised to the hospital. My aunt informed me that the fact it took them so long to get a pulse was not a good sign. We got to the hospital, and a circle of my family was inside the room, just sitting on the edge of our seats and praying for a miracle. A miracle did not occur. The doctor walked in and sadly expressed that their efforts had not been successful in recovering life in my father. He had passed away. At 3:20 in the afternoon on a warm, sunny Saturday in May, my dad left our Earth. He was fifty years old.

 The moment you know what true shock is, you cannot even express it with words. You wonder if you are living in real time. Is it a dream? A bad dream? Will you wake up? You even have dreams at night living the same moment over and thinking in your dream that it is only a dream. You look around like you are on another planet and what is happening to you right now just is not real. You almost want to touch everyone and everything around you just to prove it. It is utter misery.

THE NEW NORMAL

There is nothing that can prepare you for that new normal. The normal that never feels normal. Actually, it feels like you are the only person existing on the planet who feels like you have been through this mess of chaos and pain. The world seems like this hazy gray that once used to be an onslaught of vivid colors that shifted from blues and pinks, to calm greens and warm browns, to dark black and bleach-stricken white. The evening Dad died, I remember going to the ball field across the street and sitting on the concrete steps that overlooked the barren, grassy area, once alive with children and parents, now so lonely, with the only spectators in attendance being my mother, my sister, and me. Sitting there staring off into a field of dead memories, we discussed our disbelief and disarray of our life that we had thought was mediocre and now seemed so full and blessed. It was then that I experienced the feeling of not seeing what I had when I had it. I thought then about how money and things appeared to make one so happy and content, but in reality, it is the people that make you feel fortunate. The sharing and blending of lives together into a family unit is what builds us up. It is what fills our souls with gladness. The questions about our future now flooded our minds. *What will we do without the rock of our little family? What will we do when things break, when our cars don't run as they should, and how will we simply just go on with our lives?* The one thing we knew for sure was that we had to stick together because through our bond, we could surely keep his presence alive within our hearts.

The next several months proved to be harder than what I even realized. The shock of a loved one's death, someone who played such a vital role in your life and now is completely obsolete in your daily existence, has such a traumatic impact on your psyche. We don't really feel what we need to feel. We move through each day doing what needs to be done and giving off superficial emotions just because it is the way our mind and body respond in an effort to protect and prolong us through hardship and difficulty. I believe that God designed us this way. He made us in such a way that a supernatural nature takes over and moves us through the storm so we do not create a bigger catastrophe within ourselves. In fact, I believe that we would self-destruct, implode even within our own selves, because we were never prepared for what smashed into us. We feel like the *Titanic,* and just as the experts that designed it did not fully prepare for that one area that, if struck, would completely collapse, we may feel we are the experts on what we can handle when dealt the card, yet never saw the sliding hand that moved so quietly below and took every ounce of security out from us. At that point, that unstable and vulnerable point, you realize what you really are made of and what you can handle.

I did not handle my father's death well. I thought I did. People would say how strong I was through it, but I felt I was just wearing the biggest mask ever made. I may have not sat in a room and cried to myself, but I became this person that I did not like. I became a user of people. I looked for the attention that my dad and my former husband gave me and found scraps of it on the floor of bars and in strangers' bedrooms. Party life became the focus of my week, and my goals became achieving a list of numbers to call when I needed company to help me forget the pain I felt from my losses. The pain I felt from my damaged past. The pain I felt from never truly being acceptable to my own self.

Waking up every morning to the ticking of the clock and Mom crying in the living room, rocking in Dad's favorite recliner, became more than I could bear. I had to move out. I decided to move up closer to where I taught and discovered a refreshing change of pace for a short time. It felt good to be officially self-reliant, but I also look back on that time and feel sad that I did not realize how much I should have been there for my mother. I always needed her comfort and strength, but I was not there for her when I now can see that she needed me, even though she never voiced it. That is the feeling of regret.

CHANGES

After three months of grieving and pain, trying to find this light in the darkness, I realized I needed to make a move. I needed to move out and move on. Part of me didn't want to leave her, but I knew the best decision for both of us was to find solace on our own. So I began searching for a small apartment that I could manage to afford that was closer to my job. My standards were higher than I could be realistic about, but I was able to find a brand-new place in the town where I worked. The excitement of new living quarters always helps rejuvenate the mind and soul. I began feeling hopeful. I still remember those first months in that place. I had never experienced such independence before! However, that sadness and heaviness about my father still lingered within me. I did not know then, but in the coming months, I would face a deep confrontation with truly grieving that was going to face me. It's funny how you feel such superficial happiness about being on your own and having all the freedom of being alone, yet every night the sadness creeps back up that you are actually *alone*. My phone was my primary means of feeling the warmth of company, as I made sure to keep my dating contacts at bay. My nights were composed of disordered eating rituals and keeping up with my potential plans for the weekend. I look back now and see how truly shallow it all was. I look back and see that instead of seeking out another guy to date, I could have been reaching out to my mother and spending time with her, and investing into my memory bank with her. I still had not learned from loss. Eventually, I would learn—just not yet. I briefly dated someone that gave me the feeling of being home in my own life. Although the short time never developed into true love for me, he said those words and made me feel comfort. Made me feel a certain shallow security. Never did I consider future plans, but I was hopeful this one could be "the one." He was just different from the typical city-slicker kind of guy I kept meeting in bars or online and ending in disappointment. A week before Christmas, he abruptly broke things off. No closure, no explanation. He just needed "a break." I was infuriated by all the recent memories of his verbal outbursts—saying that he loved me and the future we had, taking me to meet his family, talking about what ifs and giving me this notion that he was solid. Broken and enraged, I began to feel this loneliness and sadness that I had never gotten to feel in the hours and days following my dad's death. I felt abandoned again! No answers why and no explanations. No signs leading up to this departure. I finally began to really feel this grief. I cried and cried. I cried hard, and I cried alone. Somehow, I still believed that I could find true satisfaction in "stuff." I stayed in that little apartment for about eight months, until I found a nicer, bigger duplex with a garage. How I missed my nice little new house that my ex had taken away from me! Finally, I was getting back to my comfort zone with living arrangements. And so I moved again, and this time, I was much happier with my little home. I enjoyed pulling into that garage and walking into my place every day. I felt this could lead to me finally reaching a happier life, which I longed for. I planned to be in this place for a good while, yet I did not know I would not be there as long as I intended. Changes were coming again for me.

As the months came and went, it was already Christmas. All I had known for the prior months were constant dating experiences and bar life. Guy after guy would come into my life for a brief moment and disappear into the trash of my "wasted time" basket of memories. What I do remember is all the loneliness that I felt, even there in that little place I now called home. I remember looking out the window and seeing the brightness of the Christmas lights decorating the empty streets and homes across from me. I remember the quiet of my surroundings. I remember being afraid of that quiet solitude. I did not like being *alone*. I thought about my mom and what she was doing. I wish now that I had gone to see her more. I thought about the happy memories of my childhood and how our family celebrated Christmastime. Ever since Dad passed on, the holidays just are never the same to me. Are they for anyone that experiences such loss with close loved ones? It is so easy to let those losses affect your current lifestyle and how you enjoy life beyond the loss. You can miss the blooming of beautiful flowers by fixating on the weeds that grow around them.

Making myself so vulnerable to love and acceptance made me hate sex and intimacy with men. To them, it may have been a purely physical and fun activity, but not to me. I played that facade and tried to be that chick who didn't care, but truly, I did. Truly, I wanted the affirmation that I could be in love with someone. I just had a wrong idea about how to achieve that love. It was not something to be earned, or rewarded with sex, and it was not something that I could practice for, but it was something that requires a genuine person, patience, and virtue. You have to accept yourself how you are, completely naked from the soul, and realize that you are enough. The old saying that true love comes when you least expect it really rings true. I think that when you are okay with who you are and what you value in life, and are not willing to succumb to pressures to be someone other than that, then the locks are unshackled and the doors are prepped and ready to welcome that love that you long to have.

I finally reached a point when enough became just that. Enough. I had lost faith in just about everything, including any kind of dating life. I started to stay home on weekends a little more, and one by one, I began deactivating myself from the circus of dating sites I belonged to. I decided to hang onto one of them, because just like a credit card, you want to hold onto at least one. As I intermittently checked my profile, I kept noticing a guy that had been viewing my profile. I noticed him on another of my former sites I had frequently used as well. Knowing how the past six months had gone with meeting potential relationships, I did not hold any hope or even much intrigue about meeting another person there. As I finally conjured up enough gumption to delete this account as well, I received a message from him. The first line read, "I noticed your profile, and I know some people you work with." Seeing that he was not too far in distance, and that he was cute, did catch my attention. After some communication back and forth, I agreed to meet him. I still recall the conversation with my sister about how I was not holding my breath on this meetup but had to at least give it one last shot. His name was Rich.

A NEWFOUND LOVE

As soon as I saw him, I felt a comfort in his eyes. I knew there was attraction there, but the comfort was different. Conversation went smoothly, and we could talk for hours upon hours. Lots of relationships begin with that initial spark, but I suppose it amounts to how much effort you are willing to extend in keeping the spark lit for as long as you possibly can. And so we continued to see one another more and more, and do the fancy date nights, but also keep many nights so simple. You know you really care for someone and want more of their time when cooking dinner together and playing catch in the backyard can be so enjoyable. It was not superficial and sex-driven, but it was substantial and enlightening. You simply feel more alive.

We met in January and continued our dating relationship well into springtime. In late spring, I found out that my mother was getting remarried. As much as I wanted to be happy, I was not completely happy for her. It had only been two years since Dad had passed, and the feeling was still fresh. I still missed his presence so much, and seeing her remarried would be a territory that my emotions had not endeavored. But alas, it was going to happen, and I needed to be there to support her. She was marrying a man named Charles. I liked him ever since I met him. He was kind and gentle. He knew Mom from a singles group, and they both were very involved in church and dedicated to faith. I trusted he was going to be good for her. I trusted her that she knew what she wanted and needed. Since he had family in Michigan, they were going to marry at his relative's home there. When I presented this to Rich, he wanted to attend with me and make a special trip out of it. The wedding was going to be in July, so it would be a great time to take a little vacation. He told me about how we could go to Niagara Falls in New York and venture onward to New York City after a short visit to view the falls. He told me the time he went was literally breathtaking and a must-see for everyone. I never had thought much about visiting there but was definitely up for the trip. So, we had a plan! It was a bittersweet feeling knowing the reason we were going was because of my mom beginning a new life, filled with new memories with someone else, but sweet because I knew excitement was in store for us in experiencing our first trip together.

There is so much anxiety that fills your soul when you begin sharing experiences with someone that could be a make-or-break deal on your relationship. You know you will have the vulnerability surrounding you because the other person will eventually see you in a raw sense. "How will we get along?" is usually one of the most primary questions you have, followed by the what-if moments. The drive to Michigan felt so short in comparison to the drive home from New York that would follow only a week or so later. I remember the beauty of Lake Michigan and the scenic views from the house where my mom and Charles would say their vows. It is such an odd feeling when you are witnessing a parent get married to another person. I don't think it matters how young or old you are—it is still an awkward thing to experience. It is like you want your parent to be truly happy, but it feels like he or she is shoving your past of only knowing the biological family unit that was your childhood and your contentment completely out the door of his or her own life. I watched her nervously get her hair done and makeup just right and take the dress off the hanger to put on and walk outside to give herself away to someone that was not my father. I was forcing myself to be okay with it, and I knew Charles was a good man, so I trusted that the best would come of her decision to remarry. If I could have done anything differently, I would have reveled in the simplicity of just being with her and enjoying the moment that was all about her. Fast-forward to today: I look back in reminiscence because had I only known that cancer would take her away in six short years, I would have savored all of those memorable moments. Moments, big or small, are all we have to carry on with the memory of those we love so much. We can never take these moments too lightly because those moments are never guaranteed with a lifetime warranty. Charles treated her like a cherished jewel, and that is what makes my heart so full. She was not only loved by us, but truly loved just as much by him.

NEW YORK, NEW YORK

After spending another night in Michigan, we would depart for Niagara the following morning. I was not sure of what to expect other than what Rich had told me, which was that Niagara was literally breathtaking. It was simply a must-see experience. As we crossed the great lake bridge, I felt anticipation of seeing the waterfalls that I had been hearing him rave over.

We checked into the hotel and quickly got settled before venturing down to the Niagara tourism area. As we strolled the sidewalks, we saw clowns showing off funny tricks, musicians playing for small crowds, and boutiques and shops getting filled by anxious tourists. As we got closer to the falls, I heard the rustling and howling of the waters that I would soon be astonished by and acquainted with. There were so many people that it was overwhelming. All of the people from all of these parts of our world just to see a couple of waterfalls is pretty amusing. You notice that all people celebrate the opportunity to capture a moment in a picture like a rare gem discovered in the bottom of an ocean. The current of the river leading over the great waterfall is so powerful but still so beautiful. It truly will consume a breath.

I followed its path as I walked along the fence that serves as the protective barrier from the powerful force of nature, and it led me to the astounding depth of the American waterfall. You cannot grasp the beauty and dominance of it in one moment. I don't think it matters what a person believes; when one comes to this source of nature, one has to start having thoughts of creation and how it began.

Niagara Falls State Park is the oldest state park in America, established in 1885 at the Niagara Reservation. Over eight million visitors explore Niagara Falls State Park annually.

We spent a while around the falls that night and decided to stop at a well-known restaurant to get a bite to eat before going back to the hotel. We decided to sit at the bar because it was so busy that night. The bartender greeted us warmly and handed us menus. Like most people in the area, we explained that we were touring and that our stay would be brief. As we chatted with her, we decided to ask where we could possibly go the following day, other than the great falls. She directed us to a hiking trail in Lewiston. The trail was along the Devil's Hole and is a five-mile trail located near Lewiston, New York, that features a river with tons of dangerous whirlpools. The trail is used for hiking, walking, nature trips, and bird watching and is best used from March until September. She explained that it could be a beautiful place to see a little extra of the Great Niagara Falls, but she was adamant that we not try to swim or get in the water. Nine years later, I can still hear her say, "Whatever you do, do not try to get in the water or swim. My best friend and I were on the trail down by the water when we were twelve, and she decided to jump in for a swim. The whirlpools in the water sucked her down, and I never saw her again."

Speechless as I may have been, I was not too worried about myself because of the simple fact that I really did not like swimming or getting wet. I was intrigued by the idea of hiking along the trail, and I love exercise, so we decided to try it the next day. Little did I know that the next day would be the most profound day of my entire life thus far. That trail would be the last place I would visit outside of a hospital for the next week.

THE DAY

The next day, we got up and headed out for the Lewiston Trail. It was a little bit of a drive, but we arrived around eleven in the morning. It was incredibly humid and hot already, and even though I was dressed in some lightweight shorts, shirt, and sneakers, I was sweating already. For lack of common sense, I decided to leave my drink in the truck. I figured we would probably find a drinking fountain if needed or we would be back in plenty of time for me to quench my thirst. We crossed the parking lot and started along the welcoming trail. The sightseeing was amazing, which overlooked the great Niagara River, and the sun was so bright that day that everything just sparkled from the top of the water. We captured a few pictures and moved along the trail. The walking path started to get a little more rough and ragged; the stairs and slopes became tiresome. Five miles is not that much, but when hiking, it can definitely be exhausting. I was getting incredibly thirsty but felt confident in my ability to keep moving. Rich had his video camera to get the different aspects of the river. We encountered a sign that pointed ahead or to the right. Ahead were more steep inclines, which were just boring, but to the right were some boulders that carried you down to the edge of the river. There sat a huge, flat (but slightly downward-sloping) rock that I just could not resist. It was like your eye moving along the wall of an art museum and all of the sudden catching a Van Gogh painting. I just had to take that right arrow.

 I started down the path, and it led me to some more massive rocks and boulders that I had to climb and stumble through, but I finally reached the flat rock that seemed to be the oracle of all the others. I stood on it, amazed at all the beauty that surrounded me. I could hear the rustling of the churning waters and feel the cool breeze they were pushing toward me. It felt amazing. I decided to venture down the rock and bent over to let the cool waters brush over my fingertips. I was so thirsty. And I was so hot. I wanted to jump in, but someone with even a small dose of common sense would not even attempt it. Although it didn't appear to be that incredibly deep, I later discovered that the gorge I was mesmerized by was 167 feet in depth. I would come to understand that in a very personal way.

 Even though it was, in reality, only minutes I spent on that rock, it felt like hours, as I decided to take it all in and sit down and relax. I watched the people over on the Canadian side of the falls just peering down at the river, and seemingly waiting for the trolley to take them across. Above me, people were enjoying the smooth ride of the trolley advancing them across the river. In front of me, the rustling waters were dancing, and I could see the *Maid of the Mist* hauling passengers over the rough waters. Rich was behind me, videotaping the views, and I could tell he was a tad nervous for me to be so much farther down the path than he was. So I stood up and asked him if he was ready to continue on, and he confirmed that he was.

Before making my way back up, I thought that I just wanted to let the coolness of the water brush my fingertips again. After all, it was not like I was trying to flirt with danger; I just wanted to admire God's creation and the beauty that surrounded me. I bent over and let the water run up just about a quarter of the way up onto my fingers. I gazed at the sparkling waves and took it in one more time. As I turned around, letting my right leg stay behind and using my left to help advance me up the rock, a minor wave came up and rubbed along the rock right behind my foot. In that very instant, I lost balance and felt my shoe slipping along the wet algae-covered rock slightly below me. I was thinking to myself, not too alarmed but completely caught off guard, that I must gain stability and use my strength to get me back onto the flatter part of that rock. The problem was that my right leg was so much farther back behind me and had no dry and concrete space to gain traction. My leg just kept sliding farther and farther back, and it was bringing my entire body with it. My body started to form into more of a curled position, trying to transfer everything in me to my core so that I might be able to still get out of this possibly tragic event. My body just kept seeping into the water slowly, but completely submissively. As half of my lower body was now in the water, I realized I had to cling to something near me so the current did not take me off. I looked at Rich, and he had a face of absolute horror at what he was observing. He kept saying to me to swim, amongst other ideas, but I could not hear him well, as the waves were so loud around me. I was being pulled farther away from the shore, and the current was taking me for a ride, whether I wanted to or not.

My whole body was submersed in the water, and all of my strength was being used to keep my head above water. I thought about what the waitress had told us, and I knew I was going to die today. The initial shock of knowing you are going to die is so overwhelming that you cannot even process it emotionally or mentally. Your body is in a complete state of survival mode, and it will do whatever needs to be done to stay alive. I believe we were created by God with these natural instincts. So although it had not fully settled within me, I realized that I still was alive and had no control over anything that was about to happen. So while I was cognizant and aware of life, I then turned to my faith. I looked up into the sky; the sun was beating onto my face as I gasped for air, the few clouds that were above were cirrus clouds, and there may have been some rain in the forecast. But I was going through a massive storm all by myself at that moment. I then thought about my dad, who had died and whom I believe is in heaven today. I said as best I could to myself and definitely in my head, "Dad, I will get to see you today. Lord, I will meet You today. Please forgive me for how I have been living. I know I have not lived a life for You." It occurred to me in those brief moments that my life had been spent wastefully and lustfully. I could not look at my life and see that there was true evidence I was a Christian and follower of Christ. I did not have proof in my life's footprints.

At that very moment, I was taken below the current, and I was almost totally out of strength. Below the water, I could feel my legs and arms in front of me, feeling branches and debris brushing against me. I could hear the bubbles of the water in my ears. It was taking me all over the river.

LEAVING ON A JET BOAT

~~

The narrative I am about to tell you from this point is based upon what I was told from various people involved in my rescue. I do not recall anything from consciousness because I was not fully conscious. After the moment I spoke to God and cried out to Him, I was taken away with the rustling waters and little oxygen at my disposal. As I was battling for air and bobbing from place to place in the current of the river, my fiancé Rich was about to encounter an opportunity to rescue me—through a jet boat.

Just as Rich was realizing that he was about to witness my drowning and the abrupt end of our relationship, the motor of a boat was coming around the bend. Niagara Falls entertains through various attractions, and one of them is the Jet Boat adventure. The boats offer a daredevil style of riding the waves of the rapids, giving their passengers a thrill.

As the boat was speeding across the river, the passengers noticed a man yelling and waving from the bank. Someone pointed. "Is he saying hi?" Another one wondered if he was just messing with them by faking an emergency. Finally, a third passenger realized he needed help.

As the boat slowed to a relaxed pace, a voice shouted from the boat, "Look, there is someone in the water!"

My head could be seen barely skimming the top of the water. Within seconds, I was sucked down again by the quick and strong current.

"Where did she go? Man! She moves fast!" Those utterances went in tandem with sheer astonishment that they, the passengers, were either going to witness a miracle or experience a traumatic observation of a drowning. Brandy was one of the boat crew that was leading the excursion that day. Little did she know that she would be involved in a crucial rescue that Monday in July when she had agreed to take on the noon shift for leading a tour on the river.

Months later, I would receive a letter from her that informed me that she had not been scheduled to work that shift that day. In fact, the person that was had an occurrence that hindered her ability to make that shift, so Brandy agreed to swap shifts. Brandy kept telling me to "swim to the line," and I cannot seem to recall any line or seeing her doing all she could to be able to grasp me from the water. I had absolutely no strength. No ability to swim. I could barely catch my breath, and my clothes and shoes felt like a thousand pounds of extra weight on my body. I was giving up because I just could not fight anymore to stay alive.

For several minutes, Rich stood alongside the bank watching the boat circling around and wondering if they were able to possibly get me in that boat. Cody, the boat captain, was making sure to drive as carefully as possible. He was fearful that I might get caught in the motor.

As the boat continued to slowly circle the churning waters, silence grew among the passengers. One of them, who was videotaping the event of the ride that day, started mumbling about how weird it was getting, the experience they were enduring, quite possibly having just witnessed a person drown right in front of them. All of a sudden, a few passengers alerted the guide that I was coming afloat, rising up to the surface with my face downward, in a "dead man's float." I was close enough that I could be hoisted into the boat. A strand of passengers volunteered to work together to lift me from the water and into the boat, thereby risking their own lives to potentially still save mine. The boat that was used that day, coincidentally, was the only jet boat of the fleet that had a flat and open surface toward the back of the boat in which a body could be laid out. As I was lifted and brought into the boat, I was told the weight of my drenched clothes and shoes were incomprehensible for my 115-pound frame. It felt even heavier in the water trying to tread to keep my head above the waves. I was laid out in the back, and the guide asked, "Okay who knows and is willing to do CPR?" She said about twelve hands went up in the air. The woman who was chosen for the job, Lucy, was a special soul whom I would have the opportunity to reunite with a few years later on. Apparently, from what I have been told, I looked very well deceased. I was blue, with no pulse, and absolutely unconscious. The process of CPR was intense and continued for several minutes. No pulse and no breath. They continued to perform compressions and breathing and waiting for some sort of response. Brandy, in utter despair, cried out to God for help, saying she just couldn't handle this. People were praying, and even more so, people that never even knew me. But what mattered is that they knew God and knew He could save me.

Within minutes, I started gasping for breath. I had a revived pulse. The boat sped off into the abyss of the waters. Rich was left in panic and terror. "Did they leave her? Did they give up and let her drown?" In a sheer panic, he started running toward the parking lot to find answers and was stopped by a park ranger and cop. They wanted to hold him and question him and make sure he stayed calm.

As the boat was traveling back to the dock, calls to emergency personnel, EMT, and company crew were being made so everything went as streamlined as possible. One holdup, or some even said a delay of as much as a minute, could have been ultimately death. Right before the boat arrived at the dock, my heart stopped again. This time, they had the defibrillator waiting at the dock to be applied to my once-again-lifeless body. My heart was restarted, and I was hoisted onto a stretcher, placed in the ambulance, and sent on my way to the nearest hospital. I recall the EMT talking in my ear, telling me to "Keep breathing—just keep breathing." I recall that I could not budge or even move my fingers or toes, or open my eyes, but I could hear. His voice sounded deafeningly loud as he gave me directives. I know he was talking in a normal tone probably, but it felt like absolute yelling in my ear. That moment I will never forget. When you lose other senses, the ones that you still have will become sharp as a two-edged sword.

ALL THE RIGHT CALLS

As I was being transported to the hospital, Rich was being held by the police and park officials. Rich felt that he needed to make the phone call to my mother about what he had just encountered. He told her that he did not know if I was alive or okay yet and explained what he knew at that moment to be true. My mother naturally panicked and was hysterically crying and praying for a miracle.

Rich then got information from the police that I had been taken by the jet boat and they were rushing me to the hospital but unsure if I was going to make it alive or not. Upon receiving the information, he notified my mother that my whereabouts were now known. With nothing else to do but worry and feel dismay, she and my stepdad began a mad rush from Michigan to St. Mary's Hospital in New York. On the way, a brutal thunderstorm impeded travel. Having to cross a great bridge, my stepdad noticed they were about to shut off traffic through the overpass until the storm subsided. They did not want to have to wait to delay their ability to see me still alive, and in those moments, they experienced a moment of grace when they were the last car allowed to pass through.

Upon their arrival at St. Mary's (which is a smaller hospital in New York), I was still in a comatose state. The hospital could keep me alive for a temporary time but did not have the adequate technology and resources that were necessary to check my overall health and whether I had brain damage, among other organ damage. The hospital that did have the resources that my situation called for was ECMC in Buffalo, New York. The ECMC Corporation includes an advanced academic medical center (ECMC) with 573 inpatient beds, on- and off-campus health centers, more than thirty outpatient specialty care services, and a long-term care facility. ECMC is a level 1 adult trauma center, including a regional center for burn care, behavioral health services, transplantation, medical oncology, head and neck cancer care, and rehabilitation; it is also a major teaching facility for the university at Buffalo. I was placed into a helicopter and transported there immediately, after only about a six-hour stay at St. Mary's Hospital. I was placed in an induced coma in order to check brain activity and trauma. I recall the night I felt some consciousness because I was being fed a comforting portion of hot soup as I sat up in the bed. I tried opening my eyes but still could hardly see. A man with long hair, who looked very much like a Native American, with long black braids, stood across from my bed. I wondered who he was and why he was there. However, still so hazy from the trauma, I did not spend much energy thinking about it. My mom was the one feeding me the warm soup; she was just like when I was a little girl sick with the flu or chicken pox, and she nursed me back to health. I sensed her lovingkindness and gentle ways, even though I could not observe the details with alertness. She told me that the Native American was actually a Christian biker who was praying for me as he was *en route* on their motorcycle travels. Apparently, his group was notified of my accident and wanted to pray for me. It was an amazing blessing.

The next time I would remember would be as I mostly regained consciousness and became more alert to my surroundings. I was moved into a different patient room with an empty bed beside me. Rich was in the room waiting for me to awaken. I was still very foggy, very sore, and very confused about all that had transpired. Most notable was the soreness of my ribs from the CPR resuscitation. I felt like a child being told a bedtime story when Rich was trying to explain all that had happened. Shortly after I was awake, a doctor came in to greet and inform me. He told me about how they had had to put me into a coma and had received positive results that my brain activity was fine and no damage had been detected. Although I was sore, the only trauma that my body experienced externally were scrapes and a few bruises from being shifted about in the water. The doctors that saw me seemed almost discombobulated that I was basically unscathed. I had this cup-like apparatus that I had to cough and spit in that would basically expose what had been in my lungs from drowning. It was brown, dirty water and was absolutely disgusting. In further conversation, I would discover that I was, at that point, the only person they knew to come out of the Devil's Hole in Niagara Falls alive.

Within about a day of my arrival at Buffalo, my phone and Rich's phone were flooded with messages, calls, and notifications. I asked him, "Is this really a big deal?"

He nodded to confirm and said, "Oh, yes. This is a very big deal."

Following the messages and calls from family, friends, and the like, I also got a surprising call from a major media source.

As I picked up my phone and answered, a lady on the other end greeted me.

"Hello, this is — with *Good Morning America,* and we were wondering if you would like to share your story with us."

Still a bit hazy mentally, I staggered through the conversation and agreed to have the show come to my hospital room to visit and interview me. I was not aware that they were also inviting the Jet Boat company owner, John, and boat driver, Cody, to meet me. During the two-hour stay, I was moved with so many incredible emotions. There are truly no words to describe the gratitude and appreciation that you have for someone who has literally saved your life. Cody could have given up on me. He could have flaked out and, in fear of possibly making a mistake, he could have done what some would have done, which would be to escape an opportunity. Instead, he grasped the opportunity by the horns and took on the amazing responsibility of saving my life and keeping those on the boat safe, as well. He was truly heroic that day. John was the owner of the company, and had he not prepared his staff so well to intervene in such a situation, I would not have survived. As Cody looked at me standing in front of him, he said to me, "It is so amazing to see someone that was so completely dead actually so alive."

After we met with *Good Morning America,* I was anxious about what my story would be like on television. As I went through the rest of that evening, I found out I would be getting a roommate. She and I had conversations about our personal stories about why we were there. I remember the next morning or so, when my piece aired on *Good Morning America,* she said to me, "Wow, you definitely have a purpose in this life." That statement was said over a number of times as people learned of my story. It helps give me the faith and hope in the truth of those words.

In the following days, I would get calls from various news stations from St. Louis and New York, wanting an interview. I was getting very anxious to be able to get out of the hospital. I would ask the doctors and plead that they let me go, trying to skip down the hallway to prove I was totally fine. Although they felt pretty confident that I was okay, they needed to observe for at least a couple more days. Finally, I was released after about three days at ECMC. I hugged all the staff who had meant so much to me during my stay. They also were heroes. It was an amazing hospital. I recall, *en route* back to the hotel, being incredibly thirsty. We stopped, and I got a slushie drink. I became so chilled that I quivered for several minutes. It was something I never had experienced after drinking a slush. It was not like a brain freeze but felt like my body was literally in a state of shock from the cold drink. I could not wait to get back to the hotel. We spent another two nights at the hotel, as we were going to be interviewed again the following morning. *Inside Edition* was another big news agency that wanted to take me on a jet boat ride to revisit the rock that I had slipped upon. I also had some additional local news stations waiting at that jet boat location that would also be interviewing me. I remember my cousin sending me a message via text, telling me that I was on the front page of *Yahoo!* that day. Still stunned, I continued to do more interviews.

The major interviews in New York commenced on Friday, July 22, and we started the exhausting drive back to St. Louis. As we made the sixteen-hour drive, few words were spoken, as we both were still in complete shock at what had happened in the days prior. We had begun the trip planning a short visit into

Niagara Falls and had been anxious to see more of New York City and then travel to Tennessee and anywhere else that might be of interest. However, little did we know we would get a short visit in Niagara that would completely change my life. I remember riding along and feeling almost translucent. I felt that I had literally and truly experienced a miraculous rescue from the God of the universe. I most definitely felt, and still feel almost ten years later, that I was in the palm of God's hand that very day. How vividly I still recall looking into the bright and searing sun's rays and crying out to God in the moments of near-death. Then I just let go. I knew my fate that day and could not grasp the reality that my life was about to end already. I reflected on those last moments, when in the event of near-death you feel like you have only seconds, but those seconds occur in true slow-motion movement. You hang onto every life-giving minute you have to speak or think your last wishes and thoughts. For me, it was that I was ashamed of the life I had been living—the selfish ambition I maintained and the careless way I executed my actions. I was sorry I had not invested more in those people I loved so much, who were always the ones that really mattered. People mattered. My hair, clothes, car, and what kind of house I lived in just didn't matter when I was about to die. I knew I needed to speak out to God and tell Him what I was sorry about and that I wished I had another chance. But then, I let go, and the rest was all in God.

BACK TO ST. LOUIE

~

Upon arrival in St. Louis, I had already made an agreement to interview with two local news stations. Two interviews were with Fox 2 and one with KSDK. Both stations were gracious in their questioning and interviewing process. I was happy to share my story in hopes of encouraging others that miracles still happen. I also was aware that there were a lot of negative opinions about my accident, and I wanted to at least clarify what really happened that day.

Being on television is not as great as it seems. The world around you all of a sudden has the bird's-eye view of your entire self. Assumptions are made, and you feel like you are in a fishbowl and unable to escape. You have to be mindful of how you explain yourself—otherwise, people make harsh judgments without any background knowledge. For example, in my interview with ABC News, I stated that the reason I even knelt over to let the water run across my fingertips was that I just simply wanted to "touch beauty." Those few words created the impression of my idiocy in trying to be a daredevil. I just wanted to feel that natural beauty that always has been run across my hand. It was like reaching the Promised Land (so to speak). It was not to attempt to do something dangerous and life-threatening. However, I read comment after comment, blog after blog, asking about how stupid I could actually be and even saying that I deserved to die! I then realized a very small fraction of what celebrities (mildly putting it) go through. Everything you say or do is examined by people who do not even know you or what you stand for. I then ceased trying to read so much that was said or even watch the news clips, because I knew the inaccuracy. The most accurate news agency that did promote my story well was Fox 2 St. Louis. She thoroughly interviewed me and did not flippantly ask me things that would over-sensationalize my story.

In December of 2011, I received a letter in the mail from Brandy, who was paramount in my rescue at the Devil's Hole. As I read the letter, she revealed some things about that day of which I, or anyone else, had not been aware. She told me how she had only been working on the job with the jetboat company for two weeks. She was not seasoned and had never experienced an emergency situation like she did that day I fell in. She told me that she was not even scheduled to work during the noon shift; on the morning of that day, the girl who was scheduled to work had been pulled over by a cop and was not going to make it in for her shift, so she proceeded to ask Brandy to cover that specific shift for her. Brandy unknowingly agreed, and she covered probably the most difficult shift she would ever work. I was filled with so much emotion in reading the letter and coming to the true realization that so much was being orchestrated that day to provide a miraculous event that would change lives. Brandy went on to do missionary work and eventually accomplished a degree in nursing.

In the following months, I had a few more television shows airing my story in accordance with the theme of their show. I was on a survival show on the Weather Channel and would hear of how people "saw me on television" the night before. What provides me satisfaction is just knowing that my miraculous tale may have reached and encouraged others in some way. I did deserve to die that day, and my life was full of pointless memories of selfishness and discontent. When I was saved on that day, I realized that life is about so much more than ourselves. My rescuers were honored in October of 2011 by the New York State Parks Police and the New York Office of Parks, Recreation, and Historic Preservation. Their heroic efforts and not giving up on the idea that I could be rescued are paramount to why I was able to survive. In March of 2016, I was able to meet someone who was a huge factor in my rescue because this woman is the one who proceeded in giving me respirations during CPR. Lucy and her husband Matt, who helped to spot me in the water and pull me up into the boat, were a couple I was blessed with knowing that day. I feel like they were placed on that boat that day for the very mission of helping save my life. They reside in Nebraska, but Lucy was traveling for a job and contacted me to say that she would be in St. Louis that month. I was absolutely elated at the news of getting to meet her in my state of liveliness and ability to thank her for all that she had done for me. The night was full of tears, and emotions ran high as we talked for hours about that day, about our faith in Christ, and about our families. That day is one that marks more significance for me than many others. Beyond that, she had paid for my meal and arranged a valet to take my vehicle, as the place we met was in a busy location in downtown St. Louis. She has given me the true sense of knowing what Jesus is all about.

I later discovered messages I had gotten via social media accounts that had been filtered to my spam box. I never knew they were there until years later, but several complete strangers reached out to me to just say how thankful they were that I had survived. They were touched by my amazing story and how obvious it was that it was truly a miracle I survived. I remember, shortly after coming home, that a nineteen-year-old Japanese student studying in Toronto, Canada, was climbing the railing overlooking the falls to get a better view. She lost balance and was swept over the Horseshoe Falls. Her body was found later by divers. This occurred less than a month after the day I fell in. I recall feeling so many emotions that were mixed. I felt guilty that I had survived and she hadn't, but I felt thankful that I had been given that second chance at life. I felt the climax of anxiety as the various news channels displayed her tragedy. The similarity of our stories was that we both made faulty choices in our actions. Just as she should not have straddled that railing, I should not have been going so close to the river.

My faith was greatly enhanced on that day. Almost a decade later, I can look back and still remember the way the sky looked, the heat of the blazing sun on my face, the sheer look of terror on my fiancé's face, and calm sense of understanding that I was really going to die that day. In those moments, I was able to reflect on my life and see that it was not what I would want it to be. I quickly skimmed through milestones in my life and memories that were filled with family and people I loved. I did not want that day to be my last, but I knew it would be. I did not save myself, even though as humans, we are created for "fight or flight"; we go into a natural survival mode, and we do whatever our bodies will allow us to do to keep our hearts beating. Yet, there is a point at which we decide that we do not have the size of the fight for the size of the dog. I knew I would not be able to outswim the overpowering forces of the current or stay above the tremendous weight of the crashing waves. I did not know a boat was coming around the bend, so I prepared myself to just…let go. I went under, and everything became dark and weightless. I did not go anywhere, nor did angels come take me to heaven for a minute or two. I was lifeless in the water and completely at the mercy of Almighty God. The next moment I awakened was to the instructions from the emergency medical technicians to "Keep breathing—just keep on breathing." I am unable to understand why some survive and others do not. But I know that we all have an appointed day that will be our last. Thankfully, July 18, 2011, was not mine, and God gave me another shot at this thing we call life. I just keep on breathing.